1/8/92

Happy Anniversary
Susan + David !
May you have
millions more !
Love,
Edie + Russ

TOKENS *of* LOVE

TOKENS of LOVE

Roberta B. Etter

Abbeville Press • Publishers • New York

This book is dedicated to my parents,
Dorothy and Robert Etter, as a token of
my love, and to my very special friends
in Czechoslovakia—Svoboda Zvítězí!

Editor: Amy Handy
Art director: Renée Khatami
Designer: Adriane Stark
Production manager: Dana Cole

Frontispiece: A stand-up valentine showing two
girls in Tyrolean dress, printed in Germany, 1920s.

First edition

Library of Congress Cataloging-in-Publication Data
Etter, Roberta B.
      Tokens of love / Roberta B. Etter.
            p.   cm.
      ISBN 1-55859-100-1
      1. Love——Folklore.   2. Charms.   3. Incantations.   4. Saint
Valentine's Day.   I. Title.
   GR460.E88   1990   90-777
   398'.354——DC20   CIP

CONTENTS

LOVE
TOKENS

Love gets its name (amor) from the word for hook (amus), which means "to capture" or "to be captured," for he who is in love is captured in the chains of desire and wishes to capture someone else with his hook. Just as a skillful fisherman tries to attract fishes by his bait and to capture them on his crooked hook, so the man who is a captive of love tries to attract another person by his allurements and exerts all his efforts to unite two different hearts with an intangible bond, or if they are already united he tries to keep them so forever.

— *Andreas Capellanus*, The Art of Courtly Love, *twelfth century*

LOVE TOKENS

The history of love tokens begins with the history of courtship. This takes us back to the animal kingdom, where Mother Nature sometimes presents a pattern of constancy that is rare among humans. The *Encyclopaedia Britannica*, which gives a long treatise on animal courtship (but nothing on human courtship), lists the following as the methods by which animals incite each other to sexual activity: "the display of bright colors or adornments, such as crests, special tactile contacts; the discharge of scents or perfumes; and the presentation of prey or of inedible but otherwise stimulating tokens."

Right: Victorians often used medieval subjects, as this Marcus Ward valentine attests.

Left: Cupids present various trinkets to a seventeenth-century lady in "Whisperings of St. Valentine," an illustration from the Pictorial World, 1876. *Above right: A pipe-playing Cupid adorns the face of this antique watch. Right: A hand-painted ceramic disk in a leather case shows Cupid and two white doves.*

There is a type of fly that wraps its love tokens in a shiny transparent envelope. Man brings presents wrapped in cellophane. Certain male birds fill their nests with useless, glittering objects they know are dear to their females' hearts. Man has sought to domesticate his flighty maiden by filling her residence with the latest in household gadgets and adorning her with jewelry.

Love tokens have taken many forms through the centuries. Some were intended to win the affection of another. Others were intended to express the feelings of one lover to another. Still others were blessed with a variety of mysterious meanings.

LOVE TOKENS THROUGH THE AGES

In the early Middle Ages the engagement ceremony was quite elaborate and included many gifts. The bride-to-be received clothing, jewelry, coins, utensils, a bed, even domestic animals. According to old Gallic custom, the fiancé also presented a pair of slippers as a symbol of domestic tranquility.

It is hard to realize today, when any display of sentiment is apt to produce a nervous giggle, how much pleasure people in earlier eras, particularly the eighteenth and nineteenth centuries, took in giving and receiving simple gifts as tokens of their mutual love and affection. "Valentines" were people, selected by

Now Valentine what d'you say?

Are you inclined to name the day?

Shall I the Bridal fetters put on

And become the slave of the

Opposite: Hand-tinted card by Windsor, c. 1845. Left: A nineteenth-century valentine proposing marriage. Above: "The Love Token," engraved after a drawing by Herbert Gandy.

various custom, who exchanged gifts. Some of these gifts were the product of months of tedious labor. Village boys toiled for hours at harvest time to create the Irish harvest knot, Scottish brooch, or English countryman's favor. Wedding favors in the form of knots—symbolizing the tie of marriage—were widely distributed.

RINGS

*T*he ring has long been used as a pledge of love; the unbroken circle symbolizes eternity. In Roman times rings were not only for betrothals or weddings but were also given by lovers to the objects of their affection. The first mention of the ring in Roman literature appears in *Miles Gloriosus* by Plautus, where it is referred to as a love token sent by a fair lady to a handsome soldier. The Romans wore the ring on the left ring finger or the right middle finger because, according to ancient Egyptian physicians, a nerve led directly from these fingers to the heart. One of the rare love tokens of early Christian centuries is a ring of Byzantine workmanship dated to about A.D. 440. It

This early seventeenth-century American needlework in the form of peas in a pod—symbolizing closeness—was probably given as a bridal favor.

Published by O Hodgson. 111 Fleet Street.

WINNING THE GLOVES.

"Winning the Gloves," 1876.

is incised with the heads of a man and a woman; their faces are turned toward each other.

The modern engagement ring is derived from these traditions, and to lose such a ring is considered a very ill omen, a portent of quarrels, disaster, or even death.

COINS

Coins were used as magical amulets and charms in England as early as the fifteenth century. Such coins—known as benders from the practice of bending them twice so they would not accidentally be used as money—were given to young ladies to win their love. Midwives also carried benders for good luck while delivering babies.

Another form of love token was also created with coins. An Englishman would burnish the reverse of a half-penny, engrave this smooth surface with the initials of his beloved, and present her with the coin. These tokens were especially popular with sailors, and it was widely rumored that many sailors distributed more than one at many ports of call.

This form of love token reached America after the

Civil War and saw its greatest popularity in the last quarter of the century. The dime was most often used because the silver content made it easily workable. The most common method of engraving the coins was to punch small holes with a steel pin, although wealthier suitors might take their coins to a jeweler or watchmaker for more elaborate decoration.

GLOVES

The lady valentines of the sixteenth and seventeenth centuries expected to be honored not by mere verse and handiwork but by substantial gifts. For centuries gloves were an expensive and elegant show of affection that signified loyalty and purity. In the days of chivalry it was customary for a knight to wear his lady's glove in his helmet and to defend it with his life. In the eighteenth century gloves were such a popular gift that from 1785 to 1795 there existed a heavy glove duty. Samuel Pepys, the famous seventeenth-century English diarist, refers to gloves in several of his diary entries. In 1661 he gave Mrs. Martha Batton "one pair of embroidered and six

Right: Elaborately decorated glove boxes were often used for presentation of this popular love token. The gloves are a rare Rimmel valentine with royal seal and are dated February 13, 1868.

Accept with love
This perfumed Glove.

ST VALENTINES

GLOVES.

Top: This seventeenth-century fork depicts Eve presenting Adam with her famous love token, the apple. Center: A pair of lovers adorn a gold spoon from fifteenth-century Holland.

Bottom: A seventeenth-century German marital gift. Collection of Galila and Jacques Hollander, Brussels.

pair of plain white gloves." Mrs. Pepys must certainly have charmed her valentine of that year, for she received "a half dozen pairs of gloves and a pair of silk stockings and garters."

LOVE SPOONS

*T*he word *spoon* became associated with love and courting in times past because spoons of the same size fit so closely together and seem almost to hug one another. Spoons suggest affinity and contact, either mental or physical, and spoons and cutlery have long been tokens of love and marital gifts. In the eighteenth century the young men of Wales conceived the idea of carving a spoon from a single piece of wood and ornamenting it by piercing the handle with geometric designs and sentimental and symbolic devices such as hearts, anchors, keys, and birds. These Welsh love spoons, as they came to be known, were symbols of betrothment and were hung in the window for all to see.

TUSSIE-MUSSIES

*T*he language of flowers and herbal symbolism can be traced back as early as the fifteenth century. During the early nineteenth century the young Queen Victoria brought this romantic communication into fashion. Dozens of dictionaries appeared to help the public learn the communication of floriography. Flowers came to symbolize the most delicate sentiments in a "silent eloquence" that was considered far better than writing.

Right: This dimensional valentine composed of flower scraps reads "May your paths be strewn with flowers" and includes a picture of a jeweled ring.

Young ladies were expected to cultivate not only their gardens but their knowledge of flower language. Young men could answer these heartfelt messages with similar tokens. Since different meanings were often attributed to the same flower in different books it was essential that floral message senders and receivers used the same dictionary.

In England the small bouquets lovers exchanged were known as nosegays; the French called them *bouquetiers*. Americans adopted the name tussie-mussie from the medieval terms *tussie* (knot of flowers) and *mussie*

(from the moist moss used to keep the arrangements fresh). Elegant holders were developed and women carried floral arrangements as commonly as they carry handbags today. The holders often had their own significance and were presented by young men as tokens of love or even as engagement gifts. They were made of gold, silver, horn, ivory, gilt, and various plates. Everything that could be used to decorate jewelry was used in decorating tussie-mussie holders.

An old English wooing token at sheepshearing time was a fragrant "clipping

Flower symbolism expressed a wide variety of sentiment. The rose, of course, stood for love, but a yellow rose signified jealousy. Other meanings included heliotrope for devotion and blue violet for faithfulness.

26

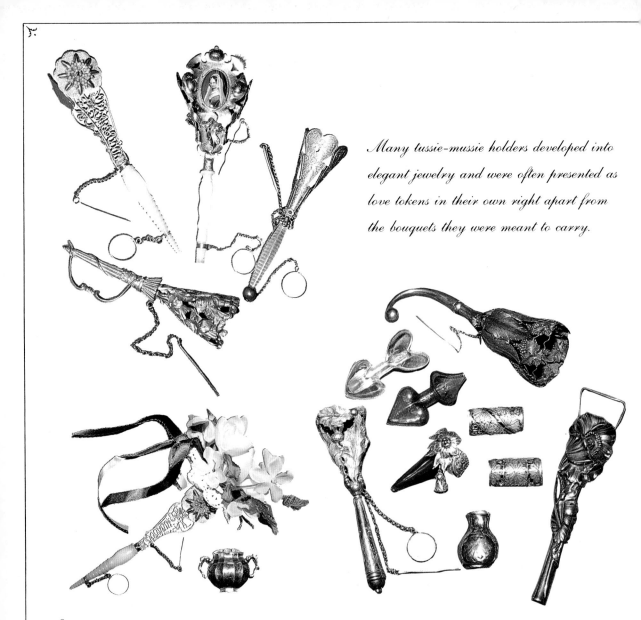

Many tussie-mussie holders developed into elegant jewelry and were often presented as love tokens in their own right apart from the bouquets they were meant to carry.

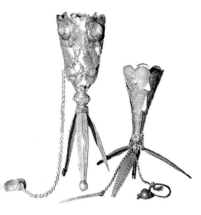

Above: Paper posy holder, c. 1910. Each of the honeycomb flowers embodies a different floral sentiment.

posy" consisting of cabbage roses, pansies, larkspur, honeysuckle, wallflowers, gorse, and lad's love. It was said that when gorse was out of bloom, kissing was out of season! Lad's love (*Artemisia abrotanum*), an aromatic cottage plant, was a powerful courting aid reputed to have special powers over women. A shy suitor could present a sprig to the girl of his choice; if she threw it down, his hopes were dashed, but acceptance meant the beginning of a courtship stroll. Honeysuckle was so strong an aphrodisiac that German parents never allowed the drowsy scent in their homes. However, English boys would bind it around hazel sticks and after several months present it to the girls of their dreams, apparently with instant success.

OTHER TOKENS

*N*eedlework tools are another important category of love tokens. Knitting sheaths, thimbles, and lace bobbins were often laboriously and lovingly adorned with hearts or other appropriate decoration. These gifts were frequently

offered during courtship, and were sometimes given as a wedding present. A bone from the meat at the wedding feast might be kept, cleaned, and turned into a bobbin. Mottoes were pricked upon the bone with a hot needle and were stained red or black, and sometimes silver or pewter was used as decoration.

A curious gift from the eighteenth-century rustic wooer was the carved stay busk, an intimate element of female attire. The stay busk was generally sewn into the corset to stiffen it, but it became fashionable for young men to carve a longer stay

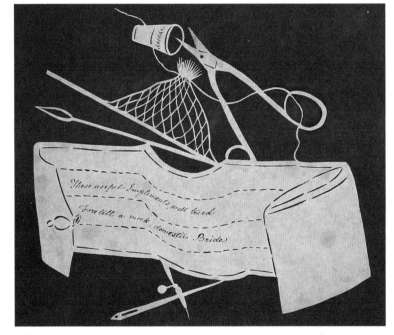

Top: A variety of intricately crafted lace bobbins. Bottom: A cut-paper love token, c. 1820, carries a portent for the future bride.

that was stitched on the outside of the corset to be admired by the recipient. Carved stay busks were made of hardwood or whale bone and were adorned with hearts, birds, flowers, and other traditional symbols of affection.

Other love tokens (suitably inscribed, of course) included decorative china, dress pins, pincushions, and snuff and trinket boxes. Glass rolling pins, decorated with flowers and initials, were also given. These delicate items, too fragile for rough-and-tumble kitchen life, were

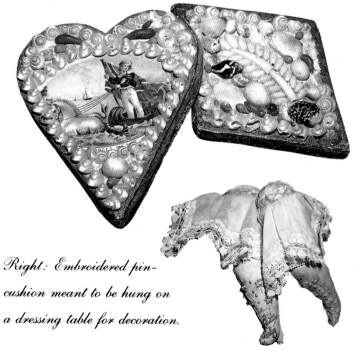

Right: Embroidered pincushion meant to be hung on a dressing table for decoration.

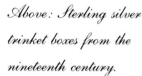

Above: Sterling silver trinket boxes from the nineteenth century.

Above: A nineteenth-century candy container. Candy has been given as a love token for the last two centuries. Left: This miniature silk violin comes complete with its own case.

hung over the fireplace as a charm to ward off witches. It was believed that a witch coming down the chimney would be compelled to count the many decorative seeds within the glass before she would be free to harm the household. Two other customary gifts were the smocked round-frock that an engaged girl would work for her future husband to wear, and the bed smoother, a large, flat disk with a heavy wooden handle. This gift, if it was intended to smooth the feathers of the bridal bed, might carry a special inscription to that effect.

Dedicated suitors often took
painstaking care to produce
such delicate cut-paper tokens.

The Urchin pulls the whirling String,
Gives the light Top it rapid fling,
And as the Play thing circles round
Delights to hear the meaning sound.

So you my fair with playful art
Still whirl in doubt your Lover's Heart
And smile to hear the wretch complain
Oh! why inflict such fruitless pain
Let Sense the light diversion stop,
Nor make the Heart as humming a Top.

A prize in any nautical antiques collection is the
"sailor's valentine." It was believed that sailors created
these tokens during their months at sea, but it is now
thought that the boxes were produced in the Caribbean
and were among the first commercial valentines.

A hand-carved sailor's love token from the mid nineteenth century.

My fond one, my true one - ere yet from the shore,
The sails shall be filled, and the tars ply the oar -
Ere the sails of your Vessel be spread to the wind,
Bethink thee the true heart thou leavest behind.

I will pray for thy welfare by day and by night -
In the darkness of storm and the perils of fight.
And all I would ask - in my fondness for thee,
Is, that sometimes thy thoughts may be wandering on me;

Farewell! gallant Sailor ! dear Child of the Wave,
In the storm none more active - in the battle more brave.
My spirit goes with thee all faithful and true,
Adoring and loving my gallant True Blue!-

I send you here a pretty toy
Which I'm sure you'll say is fine
So be a good dear little boy
And my darling Valentine

Nautical themes were extremely
popular subjects for love tokens,
as these valentines demonstrate.

Two nautically inspired pop-up valentines from the early twentieth century. The heart at the center of the windmill says, "A Token of Love."

A Token of Love

39

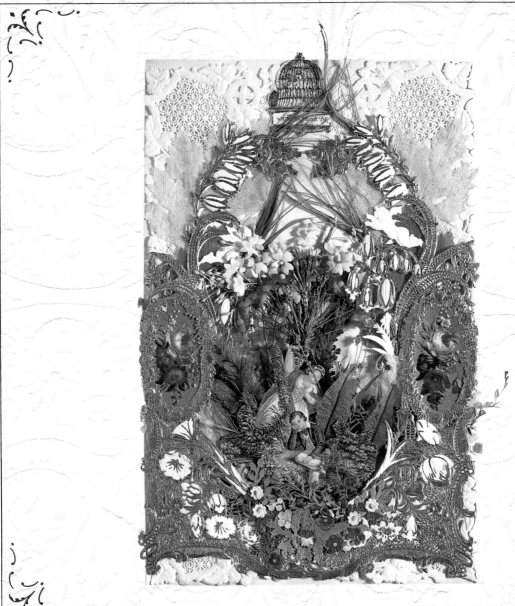

LOVE CHARMS AND INCANTATIONS

⁓

They told her how, upon St. Agnes' Eve,

Young virgins might have visions of delight,

And soft adorings from their loves receive

Upon the honeyed middle of the night,

If ceremonies due they did aright;

As, supperless to bed they must retire,

And couch supine their beauties, lilly white;

Nor look behind, nor sideways, but require

Of Heaven with upward eyes for all that they desire.

—John Keats, "The Eve of St. Agnes," 1819–20

LOVE CHARMS AND INCANTATIONS

Among the earliest forms of love tokens are those associated with the mystical power of plants, which kept a firm hold on the imagination for centuries. The garlands of oak, laurel, or olive worn by the ancient Greeks and Romans began as symbols of despotic power and came to represent military and athletic prowess. As the custom was passed to other countries, the messages conveyed by the wreaths changed. Plants acquired secular and religious significance. Holly, mistletoe, and other evergreens were brought indoors to shelter the sylvan spirits from the cold of winter. A woman who accepted the advances of a lover gave him a

Opposite: Scented valentine by Eugene Rimmel, 1870s. Pansies symbolized the loved one.

crown of birch as a token of her love; if rejected, he received a crown of hazel. The circular shape of the wreath—like the shape of the ring—symbolizes eternity, and the circle appears in many later love tokens.

THE MAGIC OF PLANTS

*M*any eras and cultures have used magic as a way to alter relations with others— particularly amorous relations—and plants were

Love rules the Court, the Camp, the Grove,
And man below, and saints above.
For Love is heaven and heaven is Love!
SIR WALTER SCOTT.

To My Own Loved Edie   J.M.E.S.'74

In Eastern lands they talk in Flowers
And they tell in a garland their loves and cares;
Each blossom that blooms in their garden bowers
On its leaves a mystic language bears.
Then tell the wish of thy heart in Flowers.
PERCIVAL

An elaborate valentine songsheet published by A. Bertini Seymour & Co., London, 1874. The tabs on the floral diecut in the center pull up to reveal floral symbolism from The Language of Flowers.

often very important elements in this process. The mandrake in particular enjoyed a widespread reputation, due to the unusual shape of the root—which suggests the human form—and the plant's potent narcotic qualities. Not only was it said to protect against battle wounds, cure all diseases, and unearth hidden treasure, but it was believed to promote fertility and to be a powerful and lucky love token. The seventeenth-century English poet John Donne declared: "Get with child a mandrake root."

In folklore as in medicine, basil had a reputation for both evil and good. It was cherished as a protection against witchcraft and as a strong lure for love. Poppies have been used by Indian women to charm unresponsive lovers, though this was considered a crime and the woman, if detected, could be expelled from the tribe. Caraway, like many favorite herbs, acquired its own folklore. In Europe popular belief held that caraway would prevent the theft of any item that contained it. This virtue gave it power as a love potion: Feed your lover caraway and he or she cannot be stolen from you.

Medieval knights emblazoned the five-fingered leaf of cinquefoil on their shields as a sign of self-mastery. Witches were said to be afraid of the herb, while sweethearts used it in love potions and divinations.

The pansy—from the French word *pensée* (thought)—served as a symbol of the loved one. As Shakespeare's Ophelia said of pansies, "That's for thoughts." Traditional flower language equates the pansy's three colors—purple, white, and yellow—with memories, loving thoughts, and souvenirs, all of which ease the hearts of separated lovers. The juice of the pansy once served as an ingredient in love potions.

LOVE IN FOLK-LORE

In the realm of love, traditions and superstitions abound. The location chosen as a trysting place carried great significance and had to be chosen carefully. Crossroads and bridges spelled bad luck, as did meeting near poplar trees, which foretold inconstancy. Instead, lovers wishing to remain true and

Arthur Hughes, The Eve of

They told her how, upon S. Agnes Eve,
Young virgins might have visions of delight,
And soft adorings from their loves receive
Upon the honeyd middle of the night,
Of Heaven with upward eyes for all that they desire.

If ceremonies due they did aright;
As, supperless to bed they must retire,
And couch supine their beauties, lily white;
Nor look behind, nor sideways, but require

Saint Agnes, 1856. Oil on canvas. Tate Gallery, London / Art Resource, New York.

Faithful, constant
and true.

The Rose

constant should meet on a hillside, by a river or seashore, or deep in a grove of trees. Seeing a white horse or a black cat when walking with one's lover augured a wonderful marriage. A girl who fell in love upstairs was said to be headed for an early marriage. The moon, too, had a role in these beliefs. Exceptional good fortune and a happy marriage could be brought about by kissing for the first time under a new moon, while, conversely, sweethearts should not look through a glass together at the new moon lest bad luck befall them.

Opportunities to catch a glimpse of one's future mate were eagerly sought. According to legend, by performing the proper magic rituals, young maidens might have a vision of their future husbands on the Eve of Saint Agnes (January 20). And charms and spells to provide premonitions of one's future beloved were widespread.

An old Arkansas charm with English origins was known as "the dumb supper" or "baking the dumb cake." Without eating or speaking for a day, two girls would bake a cake of cornmeal, salt, and springwater. Their future husbands would ap-

Opposite: "The Rose," with panel in Baxter print style. Above: The tiny envelope contains a verse about "Woman's Faith," 1840s.

49

Above: Sir Joseph Noel Paton, The Bluidie Tryst, *n.d. Oil on canvas. Glasgow Art Gallery and Museum. These lovers evidently choose an ill-fated trysting place. Right: The flowers on this 1842 valentine unfold to reveal hidden messages.*

pear as phantoms to turn the cake, then disappear through open kitchen windows. It was very important that the girls be perfectly serious, for even a laugh could destroy the charm. Similar baking ceremonies have existed the world over with varying degrees of requirements. Moroccan women were required to knead their cake dough only on their left thigh; Irish men were forced to sleep with specially prepared oranges held firmly in their armpits. Blood, hair, saliva, and urine have always played heavily in inducing true love and were often incorporated in gifts intended

for the prospective partner.

Nuts and apples have played a part in lover's magic since the days of Adam and Eve. Nuts named for lovers were placed on a hot hearthstone while on-lookers chanted, "If you love me, pop and fly,/If not, lie there silently." If the nuts jumped from the shovel to-gether, the couple was des-tined to be bound in holy matrimony.

Apple pips were used on American fires with names given for the boy and girl. If the boy's pip moved toward the girl's, a marriage would en-

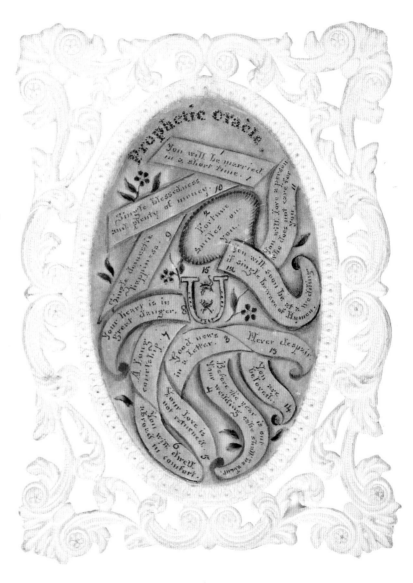

Prophetic oracle.

1 You will be married in a short time.

10 Single blessedness and plenty of money.

11 You will have a person who does not care for you.

2 Fortune smiles on you.

9 Single domestic happiness.

15 U

14 You will soon be at a wedding if single beware of Hymen.

8 Your heart is in great danger.

7 A long courtship.

6 Good news in a letter.

12 Never despair.

13 You are beloved.

4 Before the year is out your wedding will ring.

3 Your love is not returned.

5 You will dwell abroad in comfort.

A fortune-telling valentine from 1830. The numbered banners spell out love-related predictions.

sue. If the girl's moved first she was more fond of him than he of her. At social apple-paring bees the pioneer girls threw unbroken parings over their shoulders in hopes they would fall in the shape of future husbands' initials.

Many objects that had a folklore connected to divination eventually became a symbol or token of love. Stockings and garters, objects with intimate connections to their owners, were considered powerful adjuncts to divination. Shropshire servants followed this advice before going to bed on Friday nights:

This is the blessed Friday night
I draw my left stocking
into my right
To dream of the living, not of
the dead
To dream of the man I am
to wed.

Shoes were also believed to have divinatory powers:

Point your shoes toward
the street,
Tie your garters around
your feet,
Put your stockings under
your head
And you'll dream of the one
you are going to wed.

The shoes were then reversed, the lines repeated, the shoes turned again, and the verse said once more.

TALISMANS AND CHARMS

With such great superstition surrounding the plight of young lovers, it is small wonder that certain emblems became known as talismans, from the Greek word *telesma*, meaning mystery or consecration. The particular talismans dedicated to lovers have materialized in various forms for centuries. Beads were used frequently; amber beads brought luck to brides, and eye beads—shaped like eyes—were said to promote love affairs. Eye beads were often made of blue glass, since blue is the color for lovers. Other charms took the forms of fish (an ancient Egyptian charm for domestic happiness), frogs (an ancient Roman talisman to ensure mutual ardor and happy relationships), keys (a Japanese charm to bring wealth, love, and general happiness), and, of course, hearts (meant to promote constancy and joy). Another type of talisman consisted of a lock of the loved one's hair tied in a lover's knot;

To thee, my very dearest Friend,

This token of my love I send.

Come to me my pretty Dove,
And take this Letter to my love,
Tell her I hope she'll not decline
To have me for her Valentine.

Oh what is like the sweetness
Of meeting those we love!
We notice not time's fleetness,
But the height of rapture prove,
We clasp in fervid embrace
The idol of our heart
We read each others face,
And hope never more to part.

an old superstition held that keeping this would guarantee constancy. A variation on this idea was for each of the lovers to keep one half of the same sixpence that had been cut in two.

Standing stones and menhirs dating back to prehistoric times still have reputations for potency. In Ireland a woman who passes her handkerchief through a hole in the stone of Inishmore will quickly find a lover. Such stones exist across much of Europe and still draw crowds of curious followers. Tiny replicas of some of these menhirs appeared at the end of the nineteenth century and were worn as good luck tokens for love and fertility. A European custom that was passed to rural America was for a couple to visit a menhir at full moon. They were supposed to strip, chase each other naked, and then make love in the rock's shadow; this was said to guarantee a healthy crop in the fields and many sons.

Rare cobweb valentines, c. 1820s. Paper cut in an intricate pattern was lifted by a thread to reveal a hidden picture.

"You'll smile per-
haps at these your
maiden's lines/But
bear in mind
this day's Saint
Valentine's."

THE VALENTINE.

SAINT VALENTINE'S DAY

To-morrow is Saint Valentine's Day,
All in the morning betime,
And I a maid at your window
To be your Valentine.

—*William Shakespeare,* Hamlet, *c. 1601*

SAINT VALENTINE'S DAY

There were at least five saints Valentine, perhaps even seven. All accounts agree, however, that February 14 has for centuries been a day of free and often elaborate avowals of love.

The most plausible theory for Saint Valentine's Day traces its origins to the Roman Lupercalia, a feast celebrated on February 15 and dedicated to the ancient rural god Pan. During this celebration priests sacrificed a goat and a dog, then touched the blood-stained knife to the foreheads of two young boys. The boys were then compelled to laugh out loud and run through the streets, lashing out with thongs made from

"St. Valentine's Day," from the Illustrated Sporting and Dramatic News, *1882.*

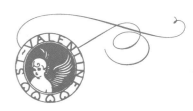

the skin of the freshly slaughtered goat. The young women they encountered welcomed the strokes, as the practice was supposed to ensure fertility.

According to some accounts, during the reign of Emperor Claudius II (A.D. 268–70) Romans were becoming weary of war. They resented being recruited as soldiers, preferring instead to stay at home with their loved ones. The irate emperor declared that no more marriages would be performed, and canceled all engagements.

Valentinus, a priest of Rome, thought this highly unfair and secretly joined several young couples. He was also reputed to have performed valiant service in assisting Christians during their persecution by the Romans. Either offense would have outraged Claudius, who had Valentinus imprisoned. Legend holds that during his imprisonment Valentinus formed a close friendship with the blind daughter of his jailor and was able to

Above and opposite: Two hand-colored engravings of Cupid, published by Edward Orme, 1807.

Blühen wird
der Liebe Rose imer
Glänzen wie der Sonne Licht
Erquikend ist wie Mondesschimmer,
Freundschaft Dein Vergißmeinnicht.

Ein froh und frei Gemüth, ein unverzagter Muth,
Macht durch die ganze Welt die schlimmsten Wege gut

A pair of uncut German valentine inserts avowing deepest love, 1810. Many valentines were printed in Germany, but valentines in non-English languages are quite rare.

restore the girl's sight. After converting both the jailor and his daughter to Christianity, Valentinus was condemned to be beaten and then beheaded. On the eve of his execution Valentinus wrote a farewell message to the jailor's daughter and signed it, "From your Valentine." The date of his execution is generally given as February 14, in the year A.D. 270.

As Christianity spread, the Church was anxious to eliminate the old pagan customs. One of the simplest ways to accomplish this was to sublimate pagan festivals by turning them into Christian feasts and to substitute a martyred saint for a pagan deity. It is thus quite possible that the death of Saint Valentine on February 14 and the feast of Lupercalia on February 15 became intertwined.

From all the splendid gay parade,
Of noise and folly free,
No sorrows shall our peace invade
My home then share with me.
A truly fond and faithful heart,
I have to offer thee,
Promise ere I with grief depart,
My home to share with me.

Part of the Lupercalian ceremony involved a type of lottery held in honor of the

ered the heathen custom of picking lots for sweethearts and at one time tried to substitute the names of saints: the youth would then be under that saint's protection for the year. But human nature intervened and by at least as early as the fourteenth century the practice had reverted to its original form, and continued in various forms as it spread across Europe, Great Britain, and eventually America. It was customary for a youth to wear the name of his drawn valentine on his sleeve. They would exchange love tokens and he was then to attend and protect her dur-

Above and opposite: Late-nineteenth-century valentines featuring bird motifs. Valentine's Day was considered the day on which birds chose their mates.

goddess Juno, where mates were selected by drawing names. Boys and girls matched during the festival would be considered partners for the year, which began in March. The Church frowned upon what it consid-

Love Birds

Oh closer bound than friend or brother
One cannot live without the other

ing the year. In some areas both sexes drew names; later only the men drew names and gave the gifts.

Another ancient belief connected with Saint Valentine's day is that it is the day on which birds choose their mates. Robert Herrick, a seventeenth-century

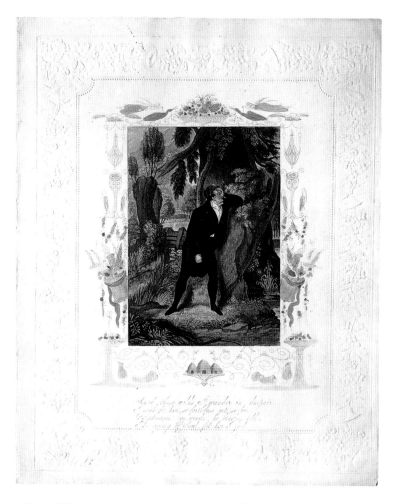

Left: "Valentine Makers." Above: A hand-colored etching from the Despondent Lover *series, c. 1820. Right: "Various Valentines," from the* Graphic, *February 17, 1883.*

English poet and clergyman, described this idea:

Oft have I heard both youths
and virgins say
Birds chuse their mates, and
couple too, this day
But by their flight I never
can divine
When I shall couple with my
Valentine.

"I got Three!"

"Poor little Dear, I know she sent it"
(But she didn't, it was only the other fellow
who shared his rooms).

Their first Valentine.

As we have seen, Saint Valentine gradually became known as the patron saint of lovers and his day became a time for exchanging love messages. Those who could write sent their loves burning words of endearment, and those who could not sent symbols and objects denoting their undying fondness for each other. Most of the ornaments were much more significant than subtle, combining elaborate arrangements of flaming hearts, mating birds, joined hands, cupids, bows and arrows, churches, rings, and various flowers.

Charles, Duc d'Orléans, is usually credited with being one of the first creators of the written valentine. From his cell in the Tower of London after the Battle of Agincourt in 1415, he sent his wife rhymed love letters in the Norman French style. The fifteenth-century English poet John Lydgate wrote a beautiful valentine in praise of Catherine, the wife of Henry V of England.

In the sixteenth century Saint Francis de Sales, a well-known dignitary and the head of the Church of England, went on record by severely forbidding and condemning the custom of sending valentines—but all in vain.

Valentine customs persisted through the years with greater or lesser emphasis placed on the actual love token depending upon one's social or financial standing. Samuel Pepys is often quoted for his references to Valentine's Day. It seems that at that time both the married and single were

"The History of a Medieval Valentine," from the Picture Times, February 9, 1856.

eligible to be drawn as valentines, a practice that could
prove quite amusing. In his
entry for February 14, 1667,
Mr. Pepys describes a
touching incident:

This morning came up to my
wife's bedside—I being up and
dressing myself—little Will
Mercer to be her Valentine; and
brought her name writ upon blue
paper in gold letters, done by
himself, very pretty, and we were
both well pleased with it. But I
am also my wife's Valentine, and
it will cost me £5; but that I must
have laid out if we had not
been Valentines.

The reference to the
cost of valentines was not
always taken with such good

*A woman dreams of her wedding in this hand-colored wood
engraving by J. L. Marks, 1860.*

humor. Couples could often find themselves embarrassingly paired. Pepys later referred to the duke of York when he was the valentine of Lady Arabella Stuart. He "did give her a jewel of about £800; and my Lord Mandeville, her valentine this year a ring of about £300."

Saint Valentine's Day was a favorite time for invoking supernatural powers to discover future events or unknown things. The *Connoisseur* of 1754 gave a wonderful account of one young lady's efforts:

THE OLD BACHELOR'S VALENTINE.

Last Friday was St. Valentine's Day, and the night before I got five bay leaves and pinned four

and took out the yolk and filled it with salt; and when I went to bed ate it shell and all, without speaking or drinking after it. We also wrote our lovers' names on bits of paper, and rolled them up in clay and put them in water; and the first that rose up was to be our Valentine. Would you believe it? Mr. Blossom was my man. I lay abed and shut my eyes all the morning, till he came to our house, for I would not have seen another man before him for all the world.

on the corners of my pillow and the fifth in the middle; and then if I dreamt of my sweetheart. Betty said we should be married before the year was out. But to make it more sure I boiled an egg hard

A young girl was eventually supposed to marry the first eligible male she met on Valentine's Day. However, if she could not stand

the suspense she could conjure up the appearance of her future spouse by going to the graveyard at midnight on Valentine's Eve. She would then sing a prescribed chant and run around the church twelve times. Those afraid to make midnight visits but still not about to leave anything to chance might take advice from a poem:

On Valentine Eve while
drinking tea,
Be sure the cat your friend
will be;
For then your future will
be bright,
Your true love you will see
that night.

There was also a belief that the first person of the opposite sex met on the morning of Saint Valentine's Day would be the valentine. Samuel Pepys noted a humorous episode when a friend, Will Boyer, arrived to challenge his wife as valentine, "she having (at which I made good sport to myself) held her hands over her eyes all the morning, that she might not see the painters that were at work gilding my chimney-piece and pictures in my dining-room." At least in this manner one might have some degree of control over the luck of the draw.

Opposite: "Where the Missive Went" (top) and "Where the Missive Ought to Have Gone," from the Illustrated London News, 1883. Below: "St. Valentine's Day" by Richard Doyle, from the Illustrated London News, 1851.

Above: "Story of an Old-Fashioned Valentine's Day" tells of eighteenth-century rivals who duel over a woman, from the Illustrated London News, 1889.

Above left: A hand-painted card from England.

Above: Valentine attributed to Esther Howland.

Right: A pair of mischievous children "tell the secret" on a card printed in Bavaria.

An assortment of chil-
dren's valentines. The bon-
net laces (top left), legs
(top center), and eyes
(lower left) are movable.

Valentine Greetings

Hear
Me,
Little
Sunbeam.
You sure will
be my Valentine.
If I have my way,
And you're going
to be All mine,
If I have my say.

To my Love

YOUR REEL VALENTINE!

Oh! Mr. Director!
Hear my cries,
Please be my Valentine
and I'll dry my eyes.

CHILDREN'S VALENTINES.

Made Expressly

For the Little Ones—having their Pets: Cats, Dogs, Birds, &c.

For Sale only by

Smith, 130 S. 11th Street,
WEST SIDE.

10c. Silk Fringed Valentines, 10c.
Over.

CHILDREN'S VALENTINES.

Made Expressly

For the Little Ones—having their Pets: Cats, Dogs, Birds, &c.

For Sale only by

Smith, 130 S. 11th Street,
WEST SIDE.

10c. Silk Fringed Valentines, 10c.
Over.

Left: A pair of stationer's trade cards, c. 1870s.

The filmmaking craze of the twenties crept into valentine design. The one at right is by cartoonist R. F. Outcault, published by Raphael Tuck & Sons.

I offer You
Without a Blush

My Heart and Hand
For I am Flush

TO MY VALENTINE

The Courier Dove.

AN OLD TIME VALENTINE.

Outstrip the winds my courier dove!
  On pinions fleet and free,
And bear this letter to my love
  Who's far away from me.

It bids him mark thy plume whereon
  The changing colours range;
But warns him that my peace is gone
  If he should also change.

It tells him thou return'st again
  To her who sets thee free;
And O! it asks the truant, when,
  He'll thus resemble thee?

Some playful valentine cards. The two shown at left date from the 1920s.

St. Valentine's Greeting.

VALENTINE CARDS

Accept this little token.
And may it speak of me;
The spell can ne'er be broken
That binds my soul to thee.

I know no form so graceful.
No face so near divine.
Then haste thee, love, oh! hasten,
And be my valentine.

— Verse from a nineteenth-century valentine

VALENTINE CARDS

By the early nineteenth century the most popular token of love was the valentine card. Those fragile paper and satin concoctions surrounded by clouds of lace could make each postal delivery a crisis. These cards take us back to the days when, from earliest dawn, noses were pressed against windowpanes in eager anticipation of the valentine bringer; back to the days when a maiden's hopes and fears were expressed in tender sighs. The fever of February 14 was deeply felt and extravagantly expressed.

Opposite: "St. Valentine's Morn: Opening the Post-Bag."

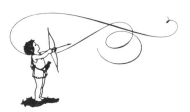

THE PICTORIAL WORLD

AN·ILLUSTRATED·WEEKLY·NEWSPAPER·

No. 102. Vol. IV. [Registered at the General Post Office as a Newspaper]   SATURDAY, FEBRUARY 12th, 1876.   **THREEPENCE.** Per Post, 3½d.

Below: "The First Valentine," from the Graphic, *February 12, 1870.*

VALENTINE MANUFACTURERS

The Victorian era witnessed the development of the valentine card into a fine art. Throughout the century the field was dominated by a handful of manufacturers.

DOBBS

Lace paper valentines of exquisite beauty were created by the Dobbs Company of England. Originally known as Dobbs Patent or simply as Dobbs, the company began business in London in 1803 as stationers and manufacturers of fancy paper. As the company grew the name was changed to reflect new ownership. In 1816 a Mr. Pratt joined as partner and the embossed mark was changed to Dobbs & Co. Dobbs and Pratt were listed as "ornamental stationers to the King" in 1824. In 1838 the imprint was changed again, this time to H. Dobbs & Co., and then to Dobbs Baily & Co. in 1845. The majority of the Dobbs valentines bear the

A rare Dobbs Patent valentine, c. 1805, with hand-painted flower.

Left: Valentine by Dobbs, Kidd & Co., c. 1851.
Above: Two looks at the manufacture of valentines.

mark Dobbs, Kidd & Co., which appeared at the time of the Great Exhibition in 1851.

Dobbs valentines were embellished with exquisite hand painting, and the central themes of flowers or cupids frequently possessed silk or satin backing. The company name, in one of its various forms, was typically embossed in minute letters beneath the central subject. American symbols proliferated, for Dobbs never overlooked the American market.

A Love Memento

Left: Dobbs, Kidd & Co. valentine, 1850. Above: Dobbs, Kidd & Co. card, c. 1851. Above right: Dobbs, Kidd & Co. valentine, c. 1850s. Below right: Dobbs valentine watermarked "J. Whatman 1848."

EUGENE RIMMEL: THE SACHET KING

Above and right: Sachet valentines, c. 1860s. Opposite: Elaborate boxed valentine by Eugene Rimmel, 1860s.

Manufacturers were constantly inventing new combinations of decorative materials and fresh devices for the most agreeable and significant presentation. During the 1860s the perfumed sachet valentine was introduced. The most popular of these were offered by Eugene Rimmel, who had headquarters in London, Paris, and New York. Rimmel was an eminent

FORGET ME NOT.

I have culled a little flower,
My messenger to be;
Let it whisper in thine ear
All I would say to thee.

Assorted sachet valentines, c. 1860s to 1870s. The flaps of the diamond-shaped one, by Marcus Ward & Co., c. 1870s, fold to create a self envelope.

Far left: The small heart with Cupid is a rare sachet valentine by Webb Millington & Co., c. 1861.

perfumer and a well-known provider of an immense variety of dainty wares catering to the pleasures of scent as well as of sight. His branches became known as "St. Valentine's Headquarters" and his floral scents were world renowned. The sachets were made of thick cotton wool and enclosed in elaborately decorated envelopes made of gilded, silvered, and embossed paper.

It would not be fair to omit mention of the important work done by other houses in their different branches of this artistic industry. Without the aid of the designer or draftsman, the lithographer, the wood engraver, the painter, the cardboard maker, or the workers in silk, feathers, glass filigrees, and lacquer, as well as others of diverse skills, we would not find these charming tokens of love today. They were simply arranged and put together with delicious fragrances by Mr. Rimmel.

Much of the gilding, silvering, cutting, perforating, and embossing that went into the fancy lacework paper was done by the George Meek firm in England. An article in the *Illustrated London News* described his operations in the 1870s:

The processes for the ornamentation of paper at Mr. Meek's establishment are first to be described. Most persons are, perhaps, aware that the gilding or silvering is done by previously putting moist varnish on the paper, and then laying gold-leaf or silver-leaf upon it, or else covering it with metallic powder. This naturally sticks to the parts which are touched with the adhesive varnish; and if that was put on, like printer's ink, by a machine supplied with a form of types or an engraved bas-relief, the letter-printing, pattern, or picture will appear in gold or silver, when the other parts of the metal-leaf are removed. They are simply rubbed off by hand, with a woollen or soft linen rag.... A ponderous machine, called a "tympan" ... reminds us of a

Near left: 1840s valentine by J. T. Wood, later called London Lace Paper & Valentine Company. Above: Delicate paper lace card.

Left: Painted, gilded, and embossed paper with attached verse. Right: Valentine by Meek, 1840s, with embossed envelope addressed to Miss Currier in Vermont.

Oh may fond Cupid touch thy heart
With his unerring magic dart,
So should I bless the hour

When Love in sport his arrow threw,
The shaft that pierced my bosom through
And placed me in thy power

steam-hammer; but the power that works it, instead of steam, is only the momentum of a huge iron wheel, having a weight of two or three tons, horizontally suspended. As the axle of this wheel rises or descends in a screw, its backward revolution, after having been wound up and raised a little, presently brings down the hammer with enormous force upon a kind of anvil solidly constructed below.

This machine is used for embossing the paper. ... After the embossing comes the process of lacing. The die, which is made of hard steel, has the paper yet sticking to its surface. It is placed on a bench, where a man with a file wrapped in sand-paper rubs away upon it, till every particle of paper raised on the protuberant points of the die is removed, leaving a number of little holes, and the remaining parts, sunk in the engraved hollow spaces of the die, form a perfect imitation of lacework. Several young women or girls are employed, lastly, in trimming and folding this ornamental paper, which is much in request for various occasions, as well as for valentine letters.

During peak seasons Rimmel hired between 80 and 150 industrious females and personally supervised them.

By the 1870s Rimmel was searching the world for innovations. He reportedly utilized the skills of Brazilian nuns to assemble artificial flowers out of the feathers of the gorgeous birds from the South American forests.

JOSEPH MANSELL

*J*oseph Mansell became involved with the manufacture of valentines around 1835. He was listed at that time as a "fancy stationer, engraver and printer." During the 1840s his work was so superior that his lace paper could be mistaken for real lace.

Mansell was particularly noted for his style of embossing referred to as cameo because the paper was so finely cut that it resembled an actual miniature. In the late 1840s he began

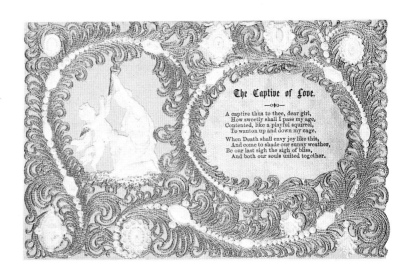

gilding and hand tinting the embossed work. Each year his embellishments became more elaborate and eventually his valentines often required boxing.

often circulated with love messages during the valentine season. The Magnus name accompanied by his Frankfort Street address appeared on most presentations.

CHARLES MAGNUS

*A*ctive between 1854 and 1870, Charles Magnus of New York City issued valentines displaying a great sense of inventiveness. Many of his offerings were of the movable variety. Handsomely decorated letterheads, stationery, and sheet music from his firm

Opposite: Cameo-style valentine by Mansell, c. 1840s. The paper lace envelope folds around the gilded insert. Above: Two pages of stationery with dimensional motifs.

Above: A mechanical card whose base wishes "Hearty Valentine Greetings." The back is signed: "To Ralph, From Ruth. Feb. 14, 1926."

Left: German mechanical valentine, c. 1920s. Right: A delicate mechanical valentine made in Saxony, c. 1912.

To my Valentine

All the mechanical valentines seen here were made in Germany. Right: The base of this little card reads: "Pretty one!/ I hope you know/This is from/Your little Beau."

Many valentines contain paper honeycombs, derived from the cobweb technique. A variety of these cards was produced in the late nineteenth—early twentieth centuries. *Near left:* A German mechanical card, c. 1910.

ESTHER HOWLAND

The pioneer spirit exhibited by Esther Howland in creating her tokens of love displayed her very strong dedication to this labor of love.

Esther's father was a well-to-do stationer from Massachusetts. In 1848 a business associate of her

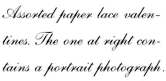

Assorted paper lace valentines. The one at right contains a portrait photograph.

Love's
offering

More examples of the ornately embellished Victorian valentine, featuring embossed paper lace, chromolithographic scraps, and gilt and silvered borders.

father sent from England a beautiful lacy valentine made on fine paper lace and decorated with colorful scraps of flowers. A small lined envelope in the center contained a tiny note expressing fervent sentiments for Valentine's Day. Miss Howland was delighted with the card and shared it with her friends. Her father, an astute businessman, watched the ladies' reactions and determined to import a few for his stationery shop. When the first shipment arrived, Miss Howland used some of her extensive artistic skill and created her own valentine samples.

Her father was very impressed with Esther's skill and enthusiasm. Her first samples were extraordinary and were sent with her brothers when they traveled on selling trips for the family concern. The first order they returned was for an amazing five thousand dollars. Rather than being overwhelmed with the work, Esther and her family seized the opportunity.

Esther hired several of her friends as assistants. She set up a large workroom in the family home and created samples for the women to copy. The small assembly line passed the

Above: Embossed valentine by George Kershaw and Son, London, 1850s.

cards from one to another and each woman added her own embellishment. Within a year Esther Howland had created a name for herself as the first commercial American valentine manufacturing business.

At the beginning the samples were only shown by her brothers, but in 1850 her first advertisement appeared in the local Massachusetts paper. Her business grew and her cards became more elaborate. It was time for her to employ some labor- and time-saving devices. She tried to have dies cut that would eliminate some of the tedious hand cutting. Though the dies were not provided, German manufacturers did create their own, and scraps were manufactured in a more convenient form for use.

Howland valentines were always top quality, utilizing the finest embossed and perforated paper lace from the best English makers. The earliest examples had delicate paper flowers glued on, with hand-painted vines and leaves. Later heavily embossed and brightly colored German scraps were used. Esther Howland is said to have been the first to use these small, colorful glazed wafers of paper to relieve the starkness of the lace

Left: Fabric leaves and paper scraps ornament this net-backed paper lace card. Above: The central motif of this tiny card lifts up for dimensional effect.

Below: The verse inside this intricately decorated card pledges: "Forget Thee, Never!"

blanks. This has been a method of identifying Howland valentines from the 1850s and 1860s.

Most of the Howland cards had a message that appeared inside on a separate piece of paper. She also introduced the "lift-up" style valentine and those of elaborate multiple layers. Her cards were usually stamped on the back with a red letter *H* in the upper or lower corner. Some have surfaced with a white heart and the *H* stamped in the center, while others had a printed label. Since her blanks were

Hand-colored valentines by Meek and Dobbs Kidd, c. 1850.

from England, the paper often bears the impression of Mansell, Wood, Mullord, Windsor, or the like. By the 1870s the business had expanded tremendously and Miss Howland formed the New England Valentine Company. Cards from this period were embossed N.E.V.Co.

During the mid to late 1870s Esther Howland was associated in business with a Jotham Taft. Tragedy befell the family in the 1880s, and Esther sold her business to attend to her widowed father, who had been critically injured in an accident. The business was sold to George C. Whitney & Co.

A classical bust and painter's palette adorn this valentine.

GEORGE C. WHITNEY & CO.

These little cards proclaim: "Yours forever" and "Sweet is True Love."

The Whitney Company was dealing with stationery and paper goods during the 1860s. They also imported paper lace and embossed envelopes from the finest English manufacturers. Early Whitney valentines so closely resembled those of Esther Howland that only the identifying red *W* on the back could distinguish them.

Whitney bought the A. J. Fisher Company of New York. Fisher had been engaged in the comic valentine publishing business since 1835, and had a tremendous stock of cuts and plates in his plant. It has been suggested that since Whitney found the comic valentine degrading he sold those plates to another New York competitor, McLoughlin Brothers. His next important career move was the purchase in 1869 of the Berlin and Jones Company, one of America's oldest and largest valentine manufacturers.

As the Whitney business grew, George Whitney became impatient with importing materials and determined that it would be financially advantageous to manufacture his own. He spared no ex-

Right: This figure brings "Cupid's Message." Opposite: The verse inside wishes "love in endless measure."

pense in acquiring the finest machinery available for embossing and for making paper lace. He also bought out many smaller valentine concerns and their stocks.

Whitney's company overcame destruction by fire and continued to thrive until its owner's death in 1915. At that time George Whitney's interest passed to his son. Warren A. Whitney, who continued the business until its liquidation in 1942 due to wartime paper shortages and business restrictions.

VALENTINE WRITERS

Many early valentines came only with outside decoration; the inside was left blank to be filled in with the appropriate sentiments of the sender. As early as 1784 the unimaginative lovelorn could seek help in the form of small, inexpensive books called valentine writers, which flooded both the American and British markets.

Valentine writers provided verses and answers for every sort of feeling, from heaven-sent love and affection to the deepest of hate and abhorrence. They often supplied a choice of answers so the receiver could reply either positively or negatively. Ideas were given for male and female,

Above and opposite: Hand-colored frontispieces of two valentine writers.

Above: Valentine writer published by Dean & Co., London, c. 1840.

young and old, many trades and professions, even for military personnel. The tradespeople's valentine writer provided verse for almost every known trade. The often doubtful rhymes do not seem to hamper the sincerity of the emotion. The grocer could croon to his intended:

Your breath is all-spice, I declare,

And you're so neat and handy,

That you're as sweet, I think, my fair,

As plums or sugar candy.

Be favourable, I emplore,

These verses kindly weigh,

And if you will my heart restore,

I'll treat you to some tea.

Please take the love that Cupid holds.

Love's sweetest fruit.

Love's choice is mine.

May our two soles be united.

OFFICIAL VALENTINES

Cupid accepts the pledge
and the ticket

Cupid a Lawyer

Repairing our marriage contract

An assortment of hand-painted tradespeople valentines on Meek lace paper, c. 1850s. Each drawer and box opens to reveal a secret message.

Among the novelty valentine ideas were the "official" valentines that sprung up in the 1840s. These took the form of bank notes, summonses, passports, and other official documents. In the United States a very decorative one-dollar note was issued on the Bank of True Love. The British counterpart, issued in the form of a five-pound note, was so remarkably real-looking that it was recalled from circulation. The post office filed complaints about

V   R

Summons to a Person charged with an Indictable Offence.

Court of Hymen } To Georgina Barthropp
To Wit } of Nelson Road Yarmouth

Whereas you have this day been charged before the undersigned, one of Cupid's Justices of the Peace, in and for the said Court of Hymen, for that you wilfully, feloniously, and designedly: waylaid, entrapped, and stole from the Plaintiff in this cause, a heart, the whole, sole and real property of the said plaintiff. Chas. Hillier

These are therefore to command you in Her Majesty's name, to be and appear on Sunday the 14th day of February at Ten o'Clock in the Forenoon, or at such other day and hour as I, the undersigned may think proper to appoint, at the said Court of Hymen, to answer to the said charge, and to be dealt with according to Law. Herein fail not at your peril.

Given under my Hand and Seal this 13th day of February in the year of our Lord One thousand eight hundred and sixty

I Love Well } Justice of the Peace
in the Court of Hymen

"Love Office Telegraphs" after they were mistaken for official use. Only very close scrutiny of the 1860 summons from I. Love Well, Justice of the Peace, reveals the humorous tone of this document from the Court of Hymen.

Examples of two "official" valentines: a summons and a "Passport through Love's Realm," 1909.

From bejeweled rings to silver trinket boxes, from mysterious talismans to symbol-laden bouquets, from embroidered gloves to the ubiquitous valentine card, as we have seen, lovers have endeavored for centuries to find ways of expressing their feelings. Perhaps if all the suitors of ages past had been gifted poets we would not have been left with such a lovely legacy; had they all been able to pour their feelings into eloquent verse they might never have been inspired to create such a delightful variety of objects to bestow upon their chosen ones. As one valentine writer declared, "Poetry is the language of love, but it is not everyone that ... can put his thoughts and feelings into intelligible verse. ... It requires a higher flight of the imagination ... fully to express all the ardour and fervency of the Tender Passion." How fortunate we are that the language of love led to the development of the language of love tokens.

Mechanical val-
entine showing a
boy in Edwardian
dress, printed in
Germany, 1920s.

Left: Hand-painted angel with harp, c. 1840s. Right: Assorted gilt and silvered valentines.

ACKNOWLEDGMENTS

A book is seldom the sole effort of one person, and this one is no exception. Each step of the way is made possible by the invaluable help and advice of many people. Though it would be impossible to acknowledge everyone individually, I especially want to thank the following people: John Grossman, The Gifted Line, Sausalito, California; Valerie Harris, Quadrille Antiques, London; Mr. and Mrs. Jacques Hollander, Cutlery Collection, Brussels; Ted Holmes, Christies, London; Hugo Marsh, Christies, London; Janet Novak, New York; Evalene Pulati, National Valentine Collectors Association, Santa Ana, California; Nancy Rosin, collector, New Jersey; Uwe Scheid, Uberherrn, West Germany; and Dorothy Veirs, posy holders, Little Rock, Arkansas. I would also like to thank my editor, Amy Handy, for all of her help and for sharing my enthusiasm in this project.

Postcard, 1910.

PHOTOGRAPHY CREDITS

The photographers and the sources of photographic material other than those indicated in the captions are as follows: Milton Heiberg: cover background, pages 11, 14, 15, 17, 21, 24, 30 (bottom), 33, 35–37, 43, 44, 49, 51, 52, 54, 55, 58, 62–64, 66, 72, 76 (upper and lower left), 77–81, 83, 88, 89 (left), 91, 92, 94–101, 106, 107, 110–12, 114, 115, 117, 119, 120, 122–25; John Parnell: pages 3, 13, 25 (left), 38, 39, 56, 57, 90, 93, 102–5; Phillips Fine Art Auctioneers, London: pages 2, 6–7, 8, 40, 48, 67, 68, 71, 76, 82, 84, 108, 113, 121, 127, 129; Ed Spiro: cover items, 25 (right), 32 (bottom), 116.